I'm talking fantastic, fabulous,

Incredible, unbelievable, mammoth,

Vast!

I'm talking astronomical, mighty,

Monstrous, universal, colossal,

Magnificent, galactical!

I'm talking BIG!

First published 2001 by
Walker Books Ltd
87 Vauxhall Walk
London SE11 5HJ

The poems in this collection have previously
appeared in *There's An Awful Lot of Weirdos in
Our Neighbourhood* (1987), *Who's Been Sleeping
in My Porridge?* (1990), *Making Friends With
Frankenstein* (1993) and *Wish You Were Here
(And I Wasn't)* (1999).

© 2001 Colin McNaughton

This book has been typeset
in Caslon 450

Printed in Hong Kong

British Library Cataloguing
in Publication Data:
a catalogue record for this book is
available from the British Library

ISBN 0-7445-8187-7 (hb)
ISBN 0-7445-8238-5 (pb)
ISBN 0-7445-8242-3 (Big Book)

DUNCE

I always try my hardest,
I always do my best.
It's just that I don't seem to be
As clever as the rest.

I'M TALKING BIG!

Colin McNaughton

Colin's Best Ever Poems and Pictures

WALKER BOOKS
AND SUBSIDIARIES
LONDON · BOSTON · SYDNEY

IF I HAD A MONSTER

If I had a monster,
I'll tell you what I'd do:
I'd starve it for a week
And then I'd set it on you!

MY BEST PAL

There's a boy in our class
Name of Billy McMillan,
And everyone knows
He's a bit of a villain.

My mum doesn't like him,
No more does my dad,
They say he's a hooligan;
This makes me mad.

Okay, so he's scruffy
And hopeless at school,
But that doesn't mean he's
An absolute fool.

He's brilliant at spitting
And juggling with balls,
And no one can beat him
At peeing up walls.

He's my best mate
And I think he's just fine,
You can choose your friends,
And I will choose mine.

TRACY VENABLES

Tracy Venables thinks she's great,
Swinging on her garden gate.
She's the girl I love to hate –
"Show-off" Tracy Venables.

She's so fat she makes me sick,
Eating ice-cream, lick, lick, lick.
I know where I'd like to kick
"Stink-pot" Tracy Venables.

Now she's shouting 'cross the street,
What's she want, the dirty cheat?
Would I like some? Oh, how sweet
Of my friend Tracy Venables.

Thanks 'Trace'

WHEN I GROW UP

When I grow up
I would like to be
Rich and famous
On TV.

When I grow up
I would like to be
A mermaid
In the deep blue sea.

When I grow up
I would like to be
A baker in a
Bakery.

When I grow up
I would like to be
An expert in
Zoology.

When I grow up
I would like to be
A professor of
Geometry.

When I grow up
I would like to be
An explorer of
The galaxy.

When I grow up
I would like to be
Given a medal
For bravery.

When I grow up
I would like to be
A miner in a
Colliery.

When I grow up
I would like to be
As big as Dad
Who's six foot three.

When I grow up
I wood like two be
A tipist or a
Sectary.

When I grow up
I would like to be
All sweet and sort
Of sugary.

When I grow up
I would like to be
A millionaire
With jewellery.

When I grow up
I would like to be
The best there is
At burglary.

When I grow up
I would like to be
A practitioner
Of dentistry.

When I grow up
I would like to be
Called "Your Royal
Majesty".

When I grow up
I would like to be
A pillar of
Society.

When I grow up
I would like to be
An ace at plastic
Surgery.

When I grow up
I would like to be
Famous for my
Poetry.

When I grow up
I would like to be –
ME!

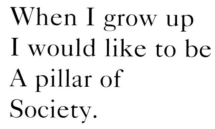

THERE'S A MONSTER IN THE NURSERY

There's a monster in the nursery,
It's been asleep all day.
It's three o'clock in the morning
And the monster wants to play!

There's a monster in the nursery,
What are we going to do?
Wash its bum and change it
'Cause the monster's done a poo!

There's a monster in the nursery,
Its howls could wake the dead!
Fetch the milk and warm it,
'Cause the monster wants to be fed!

There's a monster in the nursery,
Parents in a muddle.
What is it now? It's clean, it's fed –
The monster wants a cuddle!

There's a monster in the nursery.
It's enough to make you weep!
It's afternoon, it's time to play –
But the monster's fast asleep.

THE LITTLE MONSTER'S FAST ASLEEP!

COCKROACH SANDWICH

Cockroach sandwich
For my lunch,
Hate the taste
But love the crunch!

MUM IS HAVING A BABY!

Mum is having a baby!
I'm shocked! I'm all at sea!
What's she want another one for:
WHAT'S THE MATTER WITH ME!?

THE UN APPY BURGULLER

I'm not an 'appy burguller,
As you can plainly see,
I'm not an 'appy burguller
Cos sum won's burgulled me!

IF I WAS A BIRD

If I was a bird,
My wings I would spread,
I'd swoop over you
And plop on your head!

WHEN A DINOSAUR DAD COMES HOME FROM WORK

Be nice to Dad when he comes home
(Of course he'd never beat you!).
But if he's had a tiring day
He might just up and eat you!

NIGHT LIFE

One and two,
Baby done a poo.
Three and four,
Baby done some more.

Baby start to whimper,
Baby start to cry,
Wakes his mum and daddy up;
Mummy gives a sigh.

"I did it last, Dad,
Your turn now."
Daddy not so sure of this;
"Lazy old cow."

Daddy take the nappy,
Drop it in the bin.
Put another clean one on
And tuck the baby in.

"Nighty-night, baby,
Nighty-night, son."
Baby go to sleep again,
Three, two, one.

Daddy back in bed now,
Mummy gets a cuddle.
Baby is awake again,
Lying in a puddle.

Up you get, Mummy,
Baby done a pee.
No sleep for you tonight,
No siree!

A POEM TO SEND TO YOUR WORST ENEMY

Ugly Mug,
Fat Belly!
Slimy Slug,
Smelly Welly!

Silly Nit,
What a Pain!
Armpit,
Bird Brain!

Dum Dum,
Ghosty Ghool!
Big Bum,
Stupid Fool!

Pig Face,
Dopey Twit!
Nut Case,
You're IT!

I FEEL SICK!

Set off before dawn, sick,
    Feeling very, yawn, sick,
Wish I'd not been born, sick,
    I FEEL SICK!

Is it very far, sick,
    Ate a chocolate bar, sick,
Feeling very car-sick,
    I FEEL SICK!

Corner of my eye, sick,
    Trees are flashing by, sick,
Wish that I could die, sick,
    I FEEL SICK!

Dad says look ahead, sick,
    Wish that I was dead, sick,
Take me home to bed, sick,
    I FEEL SICK!

Queasy, woozy, hot, sick,
    My brother says I'm not sick,
Thanks a rotten lot, sick,
    I FEEL SICK!

Twisty, turny road, sick,
    Chocolate overload, sick,
Ready to explode, sick,
    I FEEL SICK!

Daddy, hurry up, sick,
    Feel it coming up, sick,
Hic! Hiccup! Hiccup! Sick!
    I'VE BEEN SICK!

P.S.

Didn't make the door, sick.
Threw up on the floor, sick.
There isn't any more sick.

I FEEL FINE!

21

MRS MATHER

Scared stiff.
Courage flown.
On that doorstep all alone.
Cold sweat.
State of shock.
Lift my trembling hand and knock.

Thumping heart.
Chilled with fear.
I hear the witch's feet draw near.
Rasping bolts.
Rusty locks.
Shake down to my cotton socks.

Hinges creaking.
Waft of mould.
A groan that makes my blood run cold.
Cracking voice.
Knocking knees.
"Can I have my ball back, please?"

ALL I ASK IS A PERFECT DAY

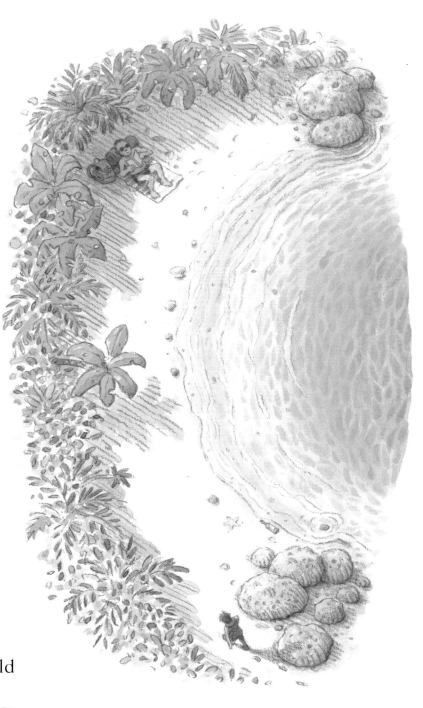

All I ask
 Is a perfect day
On a perfect beach
 In a perfect bay

In the perfect shade
 Of a perfect tree
With a perfect view
 Of a perfect sea

With a perfect breeze
 And a perfect sky
Read a perfect book
 Swat a perfect fly.

In a perfect pool
 Find a perfect shell
Eat a perfect peach
 With a perfect smell

Skim a perfect stone
 Dig a perfect hole
Catch a perfect wave
 Score a perfect goal

Make a perfect dive
 See a perfect fish
With a perfect tail
 Give a perfect swish.

Then in this perfect world
 Meet a perfect friend
And bring this perfect day
 To a perfect end.

MONDAY'S CHILD IS RED AND SPOTTY

Monday's child is red and spotty,
Tuesday's child won't use the potty.
Wednesday's child won't go to bed,
Thursday's child will not be fed.
Friday's child breaks all his toys,
Saturday's child makes an awful noise.
And the child that's born on the seventh day
Is a pain in the neck like the rest, OK!

I PLANTED SOME SEEDS

I planted some seeds
In my garden today.
They haven't come up yet,
I hope they're okay.

Should I dig them all up,
Take them back to the shop?
Ask for my money back,
Say they're a flop?

Perhaps they were faulty,
Perhaps they were duff,
Maybe they haven't
Been watered enough.

I planted some seeds
In my garden today.
They haven't come up yet,
I hope they're okay.

I hate being normal
Like everyone else.
Being normal is not
Any fun!
I hate being normal
Cos everyone knows
That two heads are better
Than one!

I DON'T WANT TO GO INTO SCHOOL

I don't want to go into school today, Mum,
I don't feel like schoolwork today.
Oh, don't make me go into school today, Mum,
Oh, please let me stay home and play.

But you must go to school, my cherub, my lamb.
If you don't it will be a disaster.
How would they manage without you, my sweet,
After all, you are the headmaster!

INDEX

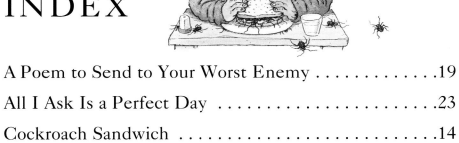

WAH!